EXTREME WEATHER JOBS

SURVIVOR SUPPORTERS

BY EMMA KAISER

WWW.APEXEDITIONS.COM

Apex is distributed by North Star Editions:
sales@northstareditions.com | 888-417-0195

Produced for Apex by Red Line Editorial.

Photographs ©: Mark Humphrey/AP Images, cover; iStockphoto, 1, 10–11, 14–15, 22–23, 24, 25, 26–27, 29; Eric Gay/AP Images, 4–5; Shutterstock Images, 6, 7, 8–9, 12–13, 16–17, 18, 19, 20–21

Library of Congress Control Number: 2023922217

ISBN
978-1-63738-921-8 (hardcover)
978-1-63738-961-4 (paperback)
979-8-89250-057-9 (ebook pdf)
979-8-89250-019-7 (hosted ebook)

Printed in the United States of America
Mankato, MN
082024

NOTE TO PARENTS AND EDUCATORS

Apex books are designed to build literacy skills in striving readers. Exciting, high-interest content attracts and holds readers' attention. The text is carefully leveled to allow students to achieve success quickly. Additional features, such as bolded glossary words for difficult terms, help build comprehension.

TABLE OF CONTENTS

CHAPTER 1

It is August 2021. **Hurricane** Ida hits the state of Louisiana. The huge storm brings heavy winds and rain. It leaves behind lots of damage.

Hurricane Ida caused $75 billion in damage.

Some hurricane winds can destroy roofs.

Many people need help. Some people's homes are destroyed. Others have lost electricity. Many people are left without food or clean water.

HURRICANE DAMAGE

Hurricanes pose many threats to people's homes. The storms can cause serious flooding. Their strong winds can break windows or knock down trees.

After a hurricane, fallen trees may block roads.

Survivor supporters travel to Louisiana. They help people find safe places to stay. They also bring food and other important supplies. They help people rebuild and recover after the storm.

Hurricanes are common in Louisiana. Support teams often bring many cases of bottled water.

CHAPTER 2

WHEN DISASTER STRIKES

Survival support teams help people after natural disasters. Some disasters are storms. These include tornadoes and hurricanes. Other disasters include earthquakes and wildfires.

Earthquakes cause the ground to shake. They can destroy buildings.

Support teams may set up places where people can come to get help or supplies.

FAST FACT

In 2022, more than 30 million people had to leave their homes because of natural disasters.

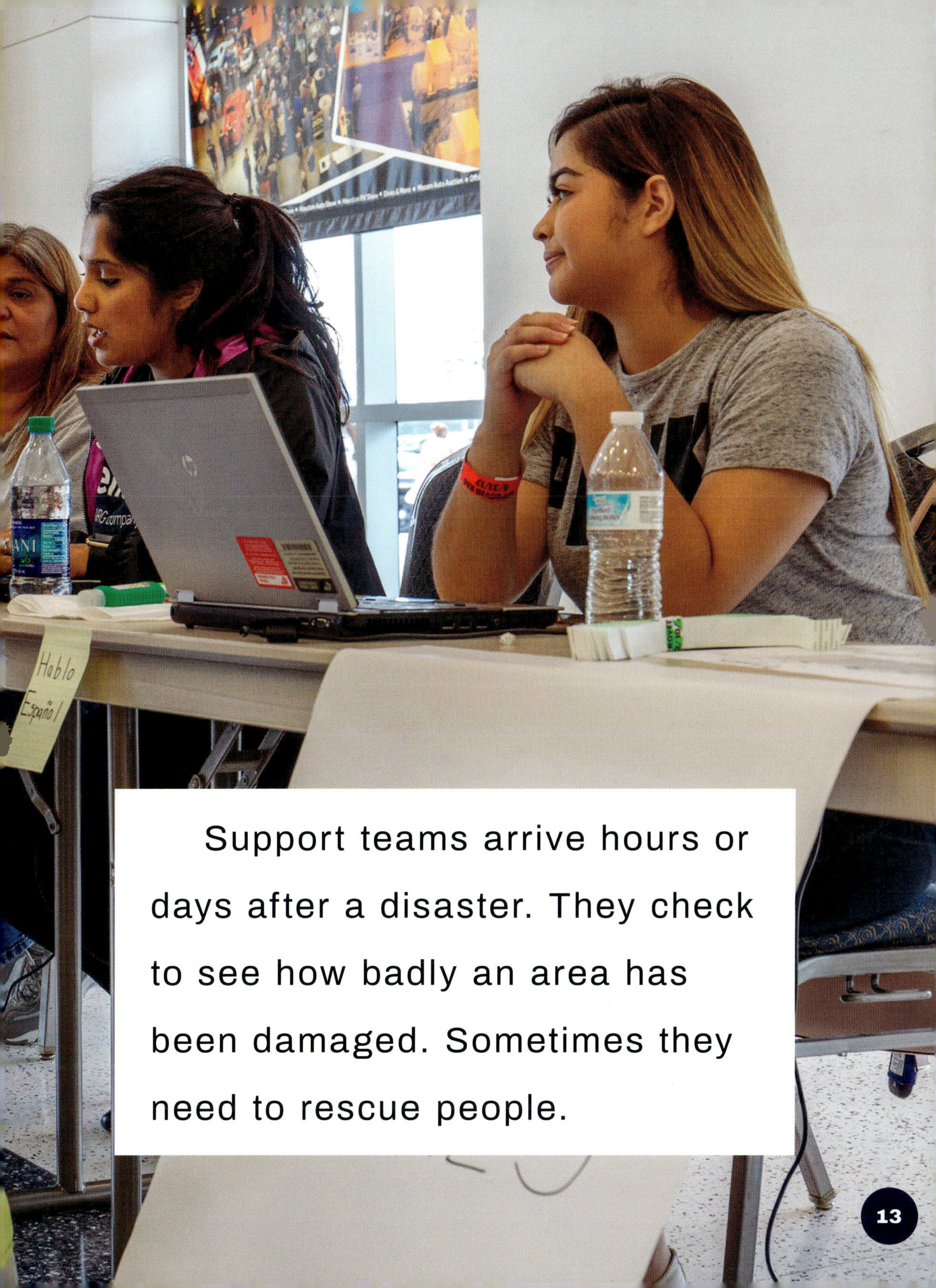

Support teams arrive hours or days after a disaster. They check to see how badly an area has been damaged. Sometimes they need to rescue people.

Haiti gets many earthquakes. Teams of doctors often travel there to help people.

Some support teams help with local disasters. Others may travel far away. They help after events in other states or countries.

AFTER AN EARTHQUAKE

In 2021, a large earthquake took place in Haiti. Thousands of people lost their homes. Many had no food or water. Support teams came from around the world to help.

CHAPTER 3

HELPING SURVIVORS

Disasters cause a lot of damage. People may need to see a doctor. So, some support workers help those who are sick or hurt. They provide care and medicine.

In 2023, natural disasters hurt more than 100,000 people around the world.

After disasters, getting and cooking food can be hard. So, some support teams serve meals.

Support teams also meet other **physical** needs. They set up shelters where people can stay. And they help people get food and clean clothes.

CLEANING UP

Natural disasters can flatten buildings. People may lose all their belongings. **Debris** may cover the ground. Support teams help clean up. They bring shovels, rakes, and other tools.

Several tornadoes hit St. Louis, Missouri, in 2011. They destroyed many homes.

People often need to fix or replace things after a disaster. Government programs give out money to help. Support teams show people how to apply for it.

FAST FACT

Some programs help people pay for home or car repairs after disasters.

Floods can sweep away and destroy cars.

CHAPTER 4

Some survivor supporters are **volunteers**. Others do **relief** work as a part of their jobs. They may work for the government. Or they may be part of groups such as the Red Cross.

The American Red Cross has been helping people in need since 1881.

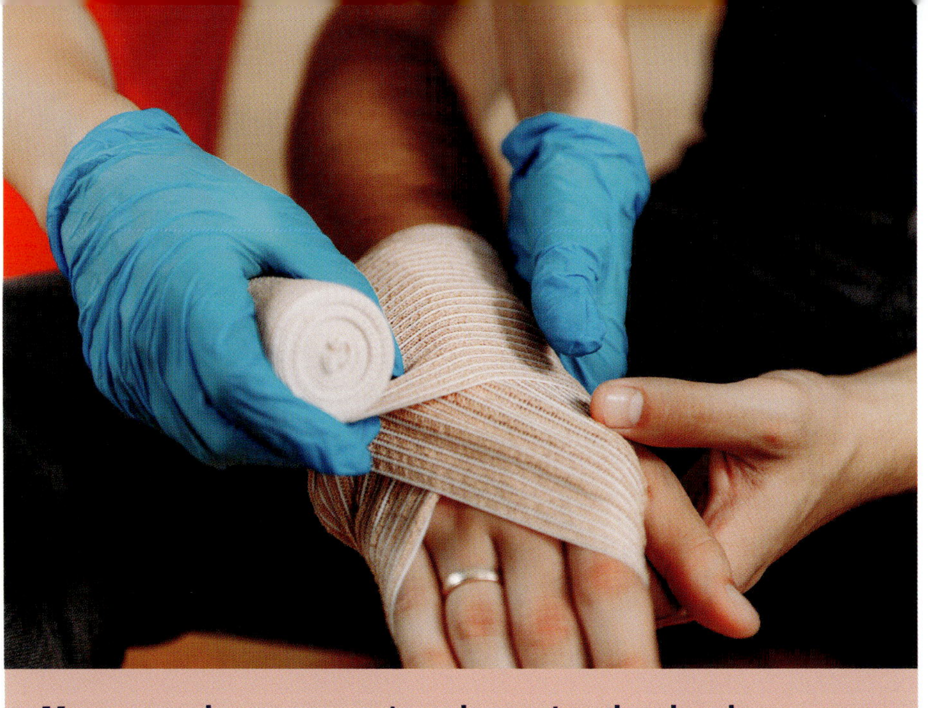

Many survivor supporters learn to give basic medical care.

Most support workers need a college degree. Some study ways to help communities survive a disaster. Many also get **emergency response** training.

FAST FACT

Some survivor supporters are trained to put out fires.

In their training, teams learn how to help when large numbers of people are hurt or in danger.

Disaster work can be stressful. Support workers must be able to stay calm. They must also be good at solving problems quickly.

OTHER EXPERIENCE

Other jobs can prepare people for survivor support. **Paramedics** know how to heal people. Firefighters have worked in emergencies. These skills are useful after disasters.

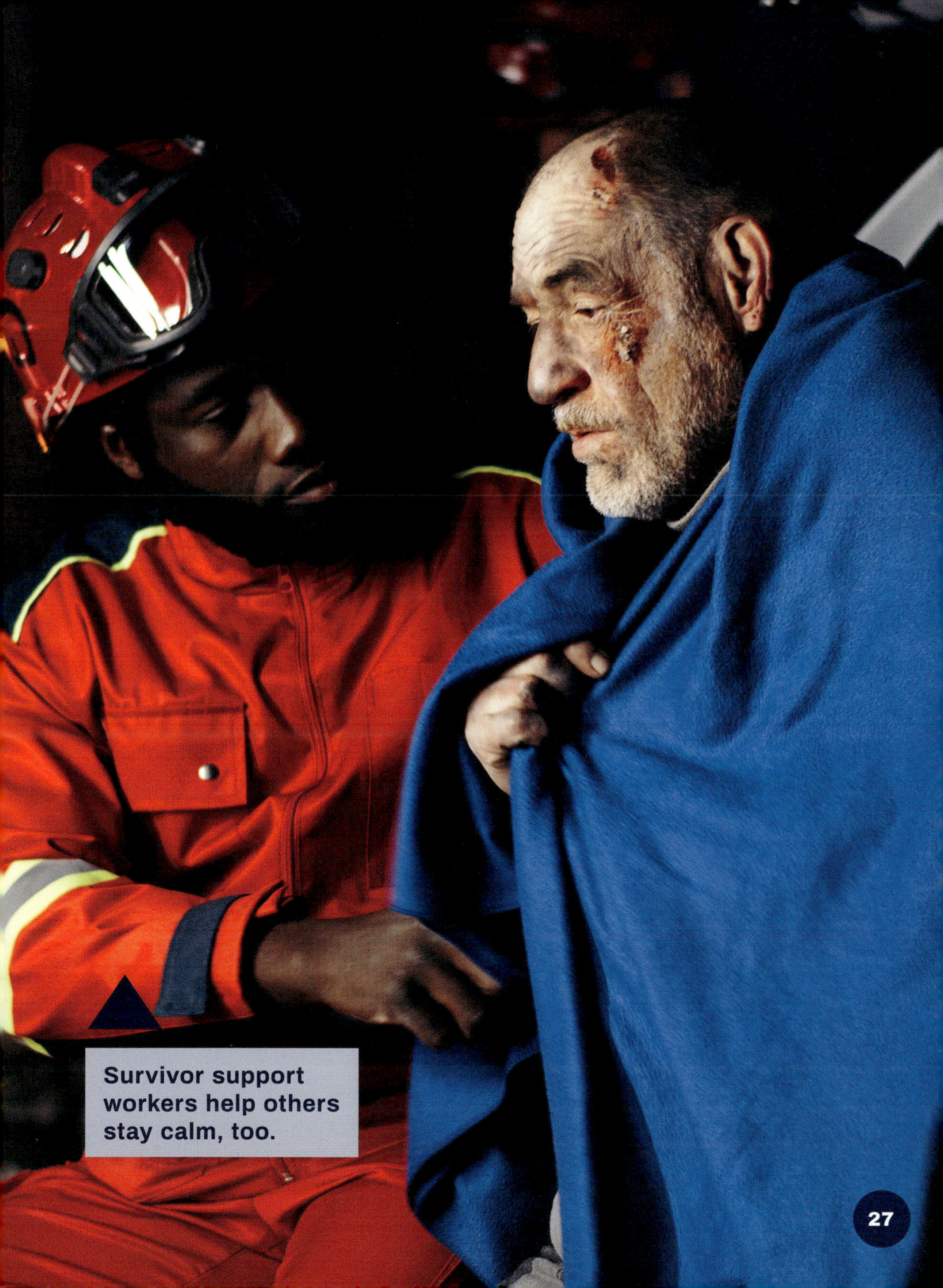

Survivor support workers help others stay calm, too.

COMPREHENSION QUESTIONS

Write your answers on a separate piece of paper.

1. Write a few sentences describing the main ideas of Chapter 4.

2. Would you want to be a survivor support worker? Why or why not?

3. Which type of disaster hit Haiti in 2021?

A. tornado
B. earthquake
C. hurricane

4. Why might people need to stay in a shelter after a natural disaster?

A. The disaster may be far away.
B. Their home may have been destroyed.
C. Their car may need replacing.

5. What does **threats** mean in this book?

Hurricanes pose many ***threats*** *to people's homes. The storms can cause serious flooding.*

A. types of fun
B. types of money
C. types of danger

6. What does **local** mean in this book?

Some support teams help with ***local*** *disasters. Others may travel far away.*

A. in a nearby area
B. in a hard-to-reach area
C. a long distance away

Answer key on page 32.

GLOSSARY

debris

Pieces of something that broke or fell apart.

emergency response

Action taken after a disaster to make sure people are safe and cared for.

hurricane

A storm with spinning winds that are at least 74 miles per hour (119 km/h).

paramedics

People who give emergency medical care.

physical

Having to do with the body.

relief

Providing help for people in need.

survivor

A person who stayed alive during a time of danger.

volunteers

People who help without being paid.

BOOKS

Crane, Cody. *All About Hurricanes*. New York: Scholastic, 2022.

Rathburn, Betsy. *Tornadoes.* Minneapolis: Bellwether Media, 2020.

Romero, Libby. *All About Earthquakes*. New York: Scholastic, 2022.

ONLINE RESOURCES

Visit **www.apexeditions.com** to find links and resources related to this title.

ABOUT THE AUTHOR

Emma Kaiser is a writer and educator based in western Minnesota. She has a master of fine arts in creative writing from the University of Minnesota, and her writing has been published in a number of magazines and publications. She is the author of several other nonfiction books for students.

INDEX

ANSWER KEY:

1. Answers will vary; 2. Answers will vary; 3. B; 4. B; 5. C; 6. A